Personality Profiles

Dream Analysis

What your dreams say about you!

Written by *Kristine Lombardi Frankel*

Introduction written by *Ariadne Green*

Illustrated by *Mark and Amy McIntyre*

B Plus Marketing, Inc.
765 Silversmith Circle, Lake Mary, FL 32746

ISBN 1-931623-07-4

Written by Kristine Lombardi Frankel

Introduction written by Ariadne Green — a leading author
and dream interpretor

Cover Design by Amy McIntyre
Illustrations by Mark and Amy McIntyre

Introduction

> *A dream that is not understood is like a letter not opened.* —*The Talmud*

You are the star, producer and director of your own dreams! Every night when you are asleep, you are sitting in the audience of a theatre called the "subconscious". A lot goes on in this theatre. Believe it! It previews and reviews your true feelings, what you really wish for, what you are afraid of, and even other people's feelings about you. Imagine that! You can know when your friends are talking about you! You rarely consider these things in your waking life because you are often too busy having fun or working hard at school. But your subconscious remembers and registers everything that you don't notice.

Every night your subconscious screens as many as 3 dreams. Each can be about 20 minutes long. Sometimes they are even longer—as long as a full-length movie. In these dreams, your subconscious plays back the tidbits of a secret life made up of feelings and attitudes that you hold inside and rarely share. Your subconscious wants you to look at yourself over and over again so that you can grow to love and understand yourself more. Even a

short feature will help you work out some of your serious problems. Hopefully, you'll feel better about yourself after a problem-solving dream. The big problems in your life such as "too much homework" or "not enough friends" need a big solution. Dreams often offer good solutions to your problems.

Dreams, just like movies, can be thrillers, action movies, nature flicks, sad dramas, or happy comedies. Once in a while you wake up with a nightmare—a terrible horror story. Scary! But one thing is true about all your dreams, good and bad. They tell you something about your life in the real world while focusing on your inner life, your truer feelings.

Dreams give good advice. If you have a bad attitude, your dream will let you know. A dream may warn you that you are making some big mistake or misbehaving. It may leave you with a message, something like "stop being so afraid of others." If a classmate bullies you at school, a dream can offer you a way to help you conquer your fear. Or it can show you that you can eventually become friends. In this way, a dream shows the potential for your future.

Although you are always the star, your friends and family shine too. They show up in your dreams a lot and play out many parts. Sometimes friends in your dreams do strange things that you wouldn't expect them to do. They can reveal parts of yourself that you may not feel comfortable with. Dreams can also show you parts that you don't let others see very often—your true personality. For example, you may wish to hug a friend to let them know that you

understand their problems. Your dream may let you do just that. Dreams also show you how connected you are to the people in your life, and how you are tuned into their feelings. Dreams can point out just how sensitive and hurt you feel when those you love have problems. But when you worry too much about friends and family, dreams can show you how overly responsible you feel. Either way, understanding your dreams helps you understand yourself and others more.

Dreams speak in a language of *symbols* and *metaphors*. A symbol represents a "big idea" that your subconscious wants you to understand. Your subconscious tells you "get the picture!" For example, a bouncing ball could represent your wish to have more fun. A metaphor gives you the details about it. An example of a metaphor in your dream might be a bouncing ball that is just out of your reach and that you can't run fast enough to catch. This could mean that your friends aren't playing with you. And that you feel like you just can't catch up to them or feel left out.

Some symbols are created by your own dream imagination. And they are surely just for you. They are what we call "personal symbols". This means that you decide what they mean. It may not mean the same thing to someone else. For example, you may sometimes enjoy a big chocolate ice cream cone with your dad on Saturday afternoon. The cone with a glob of chocolate may repeat in a dream to tell you that you wish you had more fun with your dad.

There are symbols that usually mean the same thing for most people in the world. We call these kinds of symbols of our dreams "universal symbols." All the symbols that you will have fun reading about in this book are universal.

Most people have forgotten how important dreams are. The ancient civilizations of Egypt, Sumer, and Greece used dream interpretation to heal the sick and to help people discover what the future would bring. Wise men and women interpreted the dreams of ancient travelers who needed personal advice. In our modern civilization, everyone needs good advice. Dreams still offer a lot of answers to the problems of life. All you need is some good dream magic and expert advice. Write your good and bad dreams in a dream journal. Draw a dream picture. And share your dreams with friends and your family. They are meant to help others understand you too. Using this book can help you begin to enjoy and understand your dreams.

— *Ariadne Green, Dream Educator*

"To sleep: perchance to dream: ay, there's the rub"

William Shakespeare, Hamlet (III, i)

Chapter One

Nighty-night!:

Whoa — that was a weird dream!
What did it mean?

Did you ever have a dream that you are falling and you wake up just before you hit the ground? Have you often had a fuzzy recollection about a dream from the night before, but couldn't quite remember it all? Did you ever think, "Hey, I bet that dream was trying to tell me something – if I could only figure it out?" Well, you're in luck, because this book tells you how to do just that! You'll discover how to recall your dreams, how to decipher the meaning in your dreams, and best of all, a list of common symbols (with their meanings!) that often appear in dreams.

So put on your pajamas, get your teddy bear, and start dreaming!

The Delight of Dreaming

Most of us dream only when we're asleep (except sometimes when math class gets SO boring that you have a nice daydream, right?). Dreams come to us at various times throughout the night when our sleep patterns change as the hours go by. So you might have three or four dreams per NIGHT! How are you going to remember them all?

You take notes in school so that you won't forget anything you've learned, right? Well, get a notebook and pen and put it on your bedside table. You're going to keep a dream journal.

You can use any kind of notebook for your journal, or the pages at the end of this book. You may want to use this book just for common dreams, and your dream journal for more detailed writing. And you can decorate the outside any way you want—but what matters is what's inside. Starting tomorrow morning, you're going to write down everything you can recall about your dreams. "But wait," you're thinking, "sometimes my dreams don't even make sense! How can I remember all that weird stuff I dreamt about? HELP!" OK, here are some handy tips to help you remember your dreams.

Grab your dream journal as soon as you wake up in the morning. Don't get out of bed without writing down everything you remember. You may have to set your alarm to ring five or ten minutes earlier to be able to do this, but it's worth it!

Write down absolutely everything you can remember about your dream—the people (or animals) in it, the place (or places) you were in, the colors and sounds you remember, the activities that people were doing—all of it. You want to recall as many symbols and metaphors that you can. As you write the first few things down, more memories will probably come to you. Write down everything you can recall—even if it seems insignificant. It might be important later on.

See if you can recall how you felt in a dream. Were you frightened because some scary monster was chasing you? Were you happy because you were hanging out with your best friend? Don't let scary feelings trick you into being afraid of your dreams. There are messages in even the most scary dreams. All of your feelings are very important in helping you figure out what a dream means.

If you think you might know what the dream was trying to tell you, write that down as well. You might have more insight into your dreams than you think!

OK, here's the really fun part. You're ready to take a look inside this book and find out what the symbols in your dream mean. Jot down their meanings alongside your notes about your dream. In Chapter 10, you'll find some hints to help you figure out what your dreams reveal.

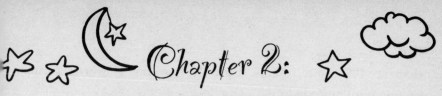

Chapter 2:

Woof! Meow! Chirp!:
What's that elephant doing in my bedroom?

Dreaming of animals can mean that you are tuned in to the natural world. The unique behaviors and characteristics of animals in the wild can teach you a lot about yourself and guide you to make personal improvements. You probably don't see tigers and dolphins in your everyday life, but you can still dream about them. Often an animal in a dream is trying to tell you something. An animal might even talk to you in a language you understand. Listen to what it has to say — it probably knows things about you that will surprise you!

Ant

Think of a colony of ants. They don't know that they're small, they don't know that they might be stepped on at any moment; they just know that they have a job to do. Tough little guys! If you are dreaming about ants, it might symbolize that you need to work hard on a particular thing. Or, it could represent a small person with lots of strength — your little brother or sister, perhaps?

Bee

Bees are busy little insects. They fly from one flower to another, bringing pollen to help the plants grow, so they can stand for hard work and success. Bees also make sweet honey, which can signify something sweet (probably not a candy bar!) coming into your life. If you are afraid of bees, one may chase you in a dream. Watch out for the sting!

Bird

Are you often dreaming about birds? Well, if you have a bird of your own, it's pretty natural that you'd dream about your pet — people tend to dream about things that are important to them. Birds usually symbolize freedom. A bird can bring a message from heaven or teach you how to really soar. Maybe you're FINALLY getting to walk to school by yourself. Or you really didn't enjoy playing soccer this year, and the season is finally over. Fly away!

Butterfly

Bet you figured this one out all on your own! A butterfly tells you that a big change is underway — just like when a caterpillar turns into a beautiful butterfly. It could be a physical change, or a mental one.

Cat

Cats traditionally represent independence. You know how cats sometimes simply can't be bothered with people? Well, dreaming about a cat might mean that you are becoming more self-reliant and less dependent on other people. Cats are also considered to be the most psychic of all animals, so you could be tapping into your psychic abilities — perhaps through interpreting your dreams!

Cheetah

The cheetah is the fastest animal on the earth. It's pretty simple to figure out the message if a cheetah appears in your dream — get moving! Perhaps you are dreaming of doing something really special, but you haven't figured out just how to do it. It's time to take some action to make your dreams come true.

Cow

Moo! A gentle cow can represent nurturing or caring. Perhaps you're in need of some kind words after really messing up on a test. A cow in a dream can also mean that prosperity and success is coming. So don't be suspicious if a Guernsey cow joins you and your family in the living room in your dream, because it might predict wealth and riches for your family in the future.

Deer

Dreaming of a deer might mean that you need to be more sensitive to others. You know how a deer hears every little rustle in the forest? Well, if you are more attuned to your friends and family, you will probably be able to understand better what they are thinking and feeling.

Dog

If you have a dog, you know how loyal he or she is! In a dream, dogs often represent a true friendship. Maybe a dog represents your best friend and the fact that you have been friends with hardly a fight since you began kindergarten. However, it might also represent you being too loyal to your friends and sacrificing your own feelings. Make sure you don't feel taken advantage of by your friends!

Dolphin

Dolphins swim in pods, and are closely connected to the other dolphins in the pod. In this way, they swim into your dreams to remind you to join your group of friends and play more. Their message is "enjoy yourself." Dolphins are also very smart, and can show up in a dream to symbolize higher intelligence.

Dragonfly

Dragonflies might look scary, but they hold a very important place in dreams. Dragonflies are the escorts, or guides, to the dream world. They tell you to cut

through illusions and to see things the way they really are — just like dreams!

Elephant

Elephants are animals that have strong family bonds, so dreaming about one might mean that you wish you were closer to your family or people in your community. Maybe you want to volunteer to help with a program at your local youth center, or perhaps you can spend more time with your brother or sister — just having fun!

Firefly

Twinkling fireflies symbolize that bright ideas are on the horizon. Perhaps you have been struggling with an idea for a report, and suddenly you have an amazing one. Fireflies also help to light the darkness, so they can show you that good things are on the way.

Fish

Dreaming of fish? Lucky you! Fish represent wealth. If you are eating fish in a dream, it can mean that you are enjoying abundance and riches.

Flea

Fleas are blood-sucking little creatures. In a dream, they may be telling you that your energy or 'lifeblood' is being sapped by others. Is someone or something wearing you down? You might need to stand up for yourself and be strong!

Fox

Did you ever hear the expression "sly as a fox?" Foxes are intelligent creatures, and if you are dreaming of one, it could means that you have to approach a problem using your head. A fox often brings the message that you are smarter than you think you are. In general, animal powers can often comment on developing a better self-image.

Frog

Ribbit ribbit! Frogs jump around a lot, so they can symbolize moving from one opportunity to the next. Maybe you just finished up with cheerleading and you're about to start track. Or you are going to a new school this year and have the chance to make all sorts of new friends. Since frogs go through big changes when they change from tadpoles, frogs also can mean that something big is coming your way that will change your life.

Giraffe

The long-necked giraffe symbolizes working towards high ideals. It can also represent the idea of having your head up and rising above a situation. Maybe your two best friends are fighting and you're always caught in the middle. Dreaming of a giraffe tells you that you need to let them work it out and not become involved.

Hippopotamus

Hippos live both on land and in water, so dreaming about them can represent the combination of your body (earth) and your emotions (water). Most often, a hippo in a dream may point to someone you know who has a big ego and a big mouth.

Horse

Horses in dreams are symbols of strength and power. Horses have the ability to take us where we want to go, and can represent the strength needed to achieve your goals.

Hyena

Did anyone ever tell you that you laugh like a hyena? Hyenas, with their cackling laugh, appear in a dream to tell you to stop torturing yourself over mistakes. Missed that big goal in the soccer game? Who cares? Hyenas tell you that thinking about old mistakes is not good — it's time to move on.

Leopard

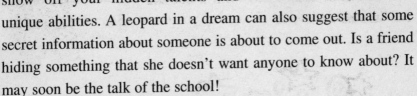

A leopard shows its spots when it comes out of hiding, and that's exactly what you should do if you dream about a leopard. It's time to show off your hidden talents and unique abilities. A leopard in a dream can also suggest that some secret information about someone is about to come out. Is a friend hiding something that she doesn't want anyone to know about? It may soon be the talk of the school!

Lion

A lion can represent a great sense of self — self-esteem, pride and happiness with who you are. But watch out! A lion can also mean that you are too full of yourself. Did you get a great score on a test and brag about it so much that your friends were sick of hearing it? You want the lion in your dreams to be a symbol of bravery and self-confidence, not an inflated ego!

Monkey

Screeching monkeys in a dream might mean that you need to express your feelings more clearly. Monkeys have strong family

bonds, so they also remind you to nurture and care for the members of your family. Maybe your little sister needs some special attention from you. But watch out! A monkey can also warn you that someone who loves to play pranks and practical jokes is near.

Mosquito

Slap, slap! Annoying mosquitoes may appear in a dream to point out that you are surrounded by other people's negativity. They could be telling you that someone is taking advantage of you (sucking your blood) and wearing you down. (See *Flea*, page 15)

Owl

This isn't too tough to figure out — an owl represents wisdom. In dreams, an owl represents the wisdom and knowledge that dreams reveal. If you are learning more and more about the language of your dreams and what they mean, an owl may appear more and more frequently to you. Remember all the owls in the *Harry Potter* adventures? Owls brought him magical power. Owls are guides to the magic of life.

Raccoon

Raccoons do whatever it takes to take care of their families. If a raccoon appears in a dream, it might mean that you need to be more resourceful in figuring out how to get things done. Maybe your budget for the school dance is a small one and you need to figure out how to stretch each dollar. A raccoon is telling you to be creative and resourceful. Raccoons are also destructive bandits. A raccoon in your dream may represent that someone entered your room without you knowing it. Check your things!

Rhinoceros

When you picture a rhino, do you picture it charging? Well, that's just what a rhino in a dream represents — a call to break through things that preventing you from achieving your goals. Maybe you need to be more assertive in trying to achieve your goals. A rhino NEVER takes no for an answer, so if you believe in something, keep pushing and see it through!

Shark

Don't be afraid of these jaws — dreaming about a shark usually means that you're responding to a fearful situation. Maybe you finally got past your fear of the dark, or big bugs don't bother you any more. Once you are past your fear, you can move on without negative feelings.

Tiger

If you are dreaming of a tiger, you could be thinking about your own personal power and how to use it. You might need to step up and lead the soccer team to victory. Or you may need to exert yourself with a friend who is overly bossy.

Whale

Large, gentle whales in a dream can signify that you are exploring your subconscious feelings. Perhaps you need go down deep into your feelings or to migrate (like whales do) to a new way of thinking. Whales sing beautiful songs in the deep blue sea. They could represent your desire to join the school or church choir.

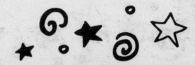

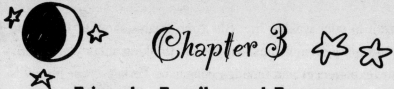

Chapter 3

Friends, Family and Famous:
J-Lo! What are you doing here?

If your friends and family often show up in your dreams, your subconscious might be telling you that you are concerned about them. By dreaming about them, you are reviewing your relationships with them so that you can make improvements. You also could be recalling good times that you had with them recently.

In your dreams, friends and family members can reveal a bit more about themselves than you ordinarily notice. Maybe they are sad and you failed to see it during the day. Other times, friends and family members act out what you believe that they are thinking about you. Think about what they are doing in your dreams, or better yet, ask them about their thoughts and feelings. People in your dreams can also show you parts of your own personality so that you can improve your self-image or look to make some improvements.

Brothers and Sisters

Because you share your childhood with your siblings (that's a fancy word for brothers and sisters!), you might dream about them quite a bit. You have a bond with them that is deep, although you probably don't

realize it in your waking life. But your dreams show it! Dreaming about a sibling often means that you are thinking about your family and the experiences and feelings you share. Perhaps your family is having some tough times, and you don't feel like you are all working together to address things. Or you have a recurring problem and your dream is telling you that it's time to fix it.

Celebrities

Are your favorite actors or singers popping up in your dreams? You may be wishing that you were like these famous people. Try to think about what is appealing about this person? Is it Alicia Keys' amazing musical talent? Or Reese Witherspoon's great style? Maybe it's time to take one of these traits and make it uniquely your own.

Father

Dreaming about dear old Dad? Think about what your father might represent: success, doing well in the world, and stability. Often fathers represent the support you need to get through tough times. Perhaps you're thinking of doing something that will mirror these traits — trying out for a new team or running for a class office. Either way, your father in a dream means that he probably has a pretty big influence on what you're doing.

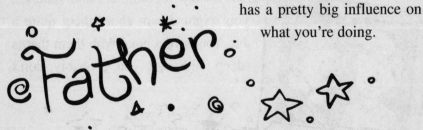

Friends

Friends in dreams aren't there just to have fun with you, although those dreams with you and your best friend at a concert are cool! They might appear to reflect traits in your own personality. Sometimes they are there to help you take a closer look at those traits. Perhaps you have a habit of being bossy — so if your best friend shows up in a dream and starts taking charge, maybe it's time to let someone else make a decision or two. Seeing your friends in a dream might also mean that you want a closer relationship with them.

Mother

"Ma! Can I have a drink of waaaaaaater?" Your mother probably brought you that drink of water countless times, and didn't think twice about it. That's just what moms do, right? Mothers in dreams represent nurturing and emotions. Maybe you need some more TLC from mom or someone else among your family or friends. Or you might need to be more in tune with your own emotions.

Chapter 4

Adventures, Athletics, Activities:
I just won an Olympic gold medal!

Dreaming about hitting the winning run in The World Series is great. But keep a close eye on the activities that occupy your dreams — you might find that your dreams are cluing you in to the best way to 'score' your goals!

Amusement Park

What do you think of when you picture an amusement park? Rides, food, and fun! You might be recalling a fun time that you and friends have shared. An amusement park in your dream might also mean that you need to have more fun in your 'real life.' Perhaps you're bogged down with homework or after-school activities and you could really use a break. Get together with some friends and take time for yourself.

Baseball

The game of baseball can represent life. You never know what to expect from the "pitcher" — it could be a curveball or a slider to throw you off balance. When you score a home run in a dream, you could be trying to complete or fulfill your destiny. Play ball!

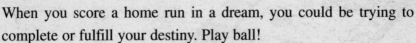

Basketball

Basketball often can represent taking aim and scoring high. Maybe your grades need improvement and you're working with a tutor to make it happen. Playing basketball in your dream may remark on an actual game you played the day before. It will let you review your shots, how well you played with your team, or whether you felt the referee was fair. Take notice and improve your game.

Bicycle Riding

A dream about riding a bicycle can mean that you are on the road to your goals. Since only you are on your bike, it can mean that you are an independent person who is moving forward using your own ideas. You may hit speed bumps, which means that the journey could be tough. Or you might be riding very quickly, which means that you are being too careless as you move along. Slow down and enjoy the ride!

Board Game

Dreaming about a board game could be sign that you're 'bored' (really, we're not kidding!) with something in your life. A board game appearing in your dreams can also be a sign that you are facing competition. It could be competition at school — like trying to get the best grade on a test. Or, it could be competition in your personal life — perhaps you feel that someone is trying to move in on your favorite boy. Keep your mind open and figure out what the real deal is.

Boogie Board

Are you riding the waves in your dream? Being on a boogie board can represent a creative wave that you are riding. Maybe you have countless ideas for new stories in your creative writing class. Or you can't stop drawing or painting. Enjoy it!

Bungee Jumping

What does it take to go bungee jumping? Bravery, right? Well, if you are bungee jumping in your dream, it can mean that you acted braver than most of your friends did in a certain situation. Perhaps you took a big risk like signing up for the talent contest. Because a bungee cord supports you when you fall, you will always bounce back if you don't succeed.

Diving (Skin Diving)

Diving in a dream is an activity that tells you that you are entering your subconscious and exploring your hidden abilities and powers. If you are encountering fish in your dive, they may be guiding the way to a 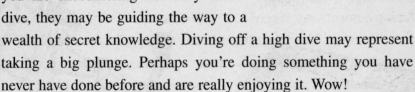 wealth of secret knowledge. Diving off a high dive may represent taking a big plunge. Perhaps you're doing something you have never have done before and are really enjoying it. Wow!

Exercising

If you dream of kickboxing and weightlifting, your subconscious might be telling you that it's time to get into shape and take care of yourself. Or it may be telling you that you need to 'exercise' your rights in a tough situation and stand up for yourself.

Football

2,4,6,8 — who do we appreciate? Are you dreaming of quarterbacks and touchdowns? If so, you may need to get a bit more aggressive in pursuit of whatever you are going after. Think of those big linebackers — they don't worry about who is in their way, they just knock them down! Perhaps it's time to take your goals a bit more seriously and start trying to make them happen!

Gardening

If you are tending a garden in your dream, it can mean that you are fulfilling your plans for the future. Gardening is hard work, and fulfilling your dreams may take a lot of energy. Different garden activities mean different things:

Watering: You're putting good energy into making your goals a reality.

Pruning: Cutting back, or pruning, means that you are paring down your ideas.

Weeding: If you're weeding your garden, you are getting rid of false beliefs that get in the way of your goals. These tasks make for a productive garden!

Mountain Climbing

Just a little further and you're at the top! Do you keep dreaming about climbing a mountain? This is a positive dream symbol — it means that you're moving towards something great! Perhaps you've been struggling in math and you finally got an "A" on your test. Whatever your goal is, you're either close to achieving it or you already have. If you have a really tough climb in your dream it means that you have a few more tough things to overcome before you finally reach your goal. You can do it!

Shopping

If you are taking over the mall in your dream, you may be searching for a new thing to 'wear' — but not clothes! Shopping can indicate that you are looking for a new way to present yourself to the world. You may be worried about a particular situation and wondering how to act in it. Try on a few new outfits and see which one fits!

Skating

A dream about roller-skating can mean that you are sailing through life without many concerns. You might be very relaxed and take things in stride. Ice-skating can mean that you are conquering your fears. Or, it can mean that you have to be balanced and poised in a tough situation.

Skiing (downhill)

Skiing down a mountain represents you conquering your fears. Perhaps you were nervous about a speech you had to make in front of a class and it went really well! Or you really wanted to talk to a certain boy and you actually did. You go, girl!

Soccer

Considering the fact that soccer is so popular these days, it seems almost natural that you would dream about it. Stepping on to the field could represent going out there and getting ready to achieve a goal. The shape of the ball combines the traditional symbols of creativity (pentagon) and productivity (hexagon), so maybe it's time for you to be both creative and productive to get to where you want to be. Score!

Surfing

The meaning of surfing in a dream is a lot like "boogie boarding." You're riding a creative wave that can move your ideas forward into a finished project. With each new wave you face, and each challenge you conquer, you have a new opportunity to be creative. (*See Boogie Board,* page 27).

Swimming

Come on in, the water's fine! If you are swimming in a dream, you're probably ready to explore your subconscious feelings. If you are dogie paddling, you may be having difficulty staying afloat because you are feeling sad. If you dream of drowning, you should share this disturbing dream with a parent or teacher. But, if you are swimming along easily, you have managed to conquer and manage your emotions.

Walking

If you're out strolling in a dream, you might be thinking about really enjoying each life experience at a slower pace. By taking it slow you can completely experience each thing that happens to you. Walking  uphill means you are experiencing your life as a challenge. And walking downhill means life is a breeze.

Chapter 5

Hair, Nails and Teeth:
Why do I dream about being bald?

Who wants to dream about a skeleton? Well, you might, if you know that a skeleton in a dream represents your innermost ideas and beliefs about life. Your may have inherited these ideas from your ancestors. They live deep inside your bones. Just like a skeleton supports your body, dreaming of one lets you examine what supports your ideas about life. But watch out — a skeleton 'in a closet' can represent something that you want to keep hidden. Check out what dreaming about these other body parts mean!

Arms

Are your arms full in your dreams? If they are, it can mean that you are presenting something — an idea, or a thought — to the world. If you have a broken arm in your dream, it can mean that you've lost your ability to reach out to other people.

Eyes

Did you ever hear the expression "eyes are the windows to the soul"? Well, that's certainly true in the case of dreams! Your eyes are what you use to see and examine the world, and in a dream, they can signify that you need to look at a person or situation more clearly. If you are looking deeply into someone else's eyes in a dream, it can mean that you are searching for their inner beauty. Are your eyes closed in a dream? Then look out — you might be ignoring something very important that you should be remembering. Did you forget about a Science test?!

Feet

Your feet are your connection to the earth and the world. They are what keep you 'grounded.' If your feet ache in your dream, it may mean that you are tired of having to stand your ground with the people you love. Or that you are just plain tired from working too hard. Maybe your schoolwork or your extracurricular activities are wearing you out. It's time to take a break, instead of breaking your foot. Because if you have a broken foot in your dream, it can mean that you are unable to move forward without help from others.

Fingernails

Your fingernails are what would be your claws if you were an animal. Animals often use their claws as protection, so when you dream about fingernails, it can mean that you are trying to protect yourself. You could be trying to defend yourself from the school bully, or you could be trying to avoid getting hurt by a friend who you think is angry with you.

Fingers

Your fingers express your talents, skills and abilities through the work you do. If you have injured fingers in a dream, it can mean that you are having a tough time at school, your job, or with an extracurricular activity. Each of your fingers has a different meaning. Your little finger represents your intelligence. Your ring finger is associated with relationships with friends, family, and others. Your middle finger relates to work and responsibility. And your index finger — your 'pointer' — is the finger of authority (picture the finger you most often 'point' with and you'll

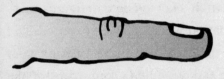

understand why!). Your thumb represents your 'grip' on the world or on the ideas of other people.

Hair

In dreams, hair represents power. If you're styling your hair, it means that you are working on and learning about your own powers. If your hair is falling out, you might be worrying that you are losing some power. Perhaps you are concerned about being a good captain to your softball team. Or you want to make sure that the study group you're in does things your way!

Hands

Help is on the way! A hand reaching out to you in your dream may mention that you are in need of help. And you just might get it if you ask the right person. Your right hand represents giving help to someone, and your left represents receiving help from another person. Shaking hands in your dream may comment on having made a new friend recently or that you should be congratulated for a job well done.

Being Naked

Lots of people have this dream. It's not too hard to figure out — it means that you were in a situation where you felt exposed. Did your friend tell a certain boy that you like him? Perhaps your teacher called on you in class and you didn't know any of the answers to her questions. Whatever it was, let's hope it doesn't happen again!

Nose

Your nose represents your ability to 'sniff out' the truth. A really big nose could mean that you are being nosy, snooping around where you are not welcome. Back off! A long nose may suggest  that someone you know has been caught in a lie. If you encounter someone with a crooked nose, it could mean that this person is telling you that something fishy is going on. A runny nose may mean you have some grief to release.

Teeth

Did you ever have that common dream that your teeth are falling out? Whoa — that's a creepy one. A dream like this might mean that you feel helpless. Are you having a really tough time talking to your best friend — you just can't seem to communicate what's on your mind? Maybe it's time for you to take a break and a deep breath and step back. Try to figure out what's bothering you and see if you can fix it.

Chapter 6:

Weather, Nature, and Disasters:

It's raining, it's pouring —

Sunshine-filled days are great in your waking life — but in your dreams, it's often the stormy days that are the most interesting. A lot of these symbols point to your innermost feelings and help you discover new things about yourself. Don't worry — these symbols won't leave you snowbound!

Air

Are you dreaming of a strong wind? If you are, a change is on the way. The change is probably in your thoughts and feelings about something.

Clouds

A cloudy day can put you in a bad mood, right? Well, that's just what dark clouds in a dream can represent. You probably feel very down about something if you're dreaming of a cloudy sky. A blue sky with no clouds can mean that your attitude about something is improving. Is cleaning your room not as bad as you thought it would be?!

Fire

Dreaming about fire is scary, right? Dreaming about a fire in your house can mean that things at home are not so great right now. Fire can also mean that you or someone close to you is being destructive with their anger and destroying relationships, just like fire destroys everything in its path. Share this dream with your parents — they can probably help figure out what's bothering you.

Flowers

Flowers in a dream represent beauty. There are many different kinds of flowers, just like there are many different kinds of beauty. You probably have a variety of beautiful characteristics that you need to appreciate. If your garden needs tending, it might mean that you have negative ideas about your beauty. So get out that rake and start weeding!

Hail

Being caught in a hailstorm can mean that you are very frightened of something. It can also signify that you were in a situation where other people's thoughts and ideas were being thrown at you. Maybe you had a student council meeting where no one agreed with you. Or you have an idea for a group project that no one in your group seems to like.

Hurricane

When a hurricane hits, it usually destroys everything it touches. When you're dreaming of a hurricane, it can mean that there is something HUGE that is bothering you. This is a great dream to share with your parents so that you can figure out what is on your mind.

Moon

The moon in a dream signifies your creative side. It may reflect on your hidden emotions and your strong intuition.

Ocean

If you are dreaming of swimming in the ocean, it can signify that you are recognizing the power of your subconscious (maybe by interpreting your dreams!). A calm ocean represents peace and serenity. If you are in a stormy, rough sea, if can mean that you have feelings about something that you need to examine more closely. Waves can represent the creative power and potential you have. Ride the wave!

Rain

Rain in a dream signifies cleansing — just like the world seems cleaner after a long rainstorm. You might be expressing your feelings about something where before you held back.

Snow

"It's snowing. School's closed, right?" Dreaming of snow can mean that you are at peace, just like the earth seems peaceful with a blanket of snow on it. On the other hand, a dream in the dead of winter with lots of frozen snow may remark that you feel someone is treating you coldly by not considering your feelings.

Sun

The sun represents light — and the source of light within you. Bet you figured out what a rising and setting sun signifies! A rising sun represents something new in your life. And a setting sun suggests that something is about to end. The sun signifies the part of you that seeks and finds answers using the logical mind.

Thunderstorm

Crash! A big clap of thunder can warn you of events that are usually beyond your control. Maybe the Britney Spears concert in your hometown was canceled and you had front-row seats. Or someone broke into your school locker. Thunder in a dream may also announce that a big emotional storm is brewing around you. Maybe everyone around you is fighting this week about the stupidest things. Don't fret — there could be wonderful things coming your way after the storm clears!

Chapter 7

Creatures, Real and Imagined:
Is that a T-Rex or a Stegosaurus?

You may think that you don't believe in aliens, but if you dream about them, part of you probably thinks that we are not alone. It's amazing what your dreams can tell you, right? The characters in this chapter tell you all different things about what's going on in your subconscious and clue you into things in your personality. Check it out!

Aladdin

Remember what happened when Aladdin found the magical lamp? He got his wish! Running into Aladdin in a dream may mean that a wish you made is about to come true.

Aliens

Aliens in dreams can represent the idea that we are not alone in the universe. But if you see a lot of aliens in a dream, you might feel like you are the different one. Perhaps you feel left out of a social situation with your friends. Or you just moved and don't know anyone at your new school.

Angel

Angels in a dream can open your heart to new feelings. They often are in dreams when you are upset about something. Did you have a terrible fight with a friend? Or are you worried about a sick relative? Angels often appear to offer comfort.

Bugs Bunny

Bugs doesn't take life too seriously. He always finds himself in strange situations, but is able to laugh his way out of it. If you're dreaming of Bugs Bunny, he may have popped up to mirror a part of you that rolls with the punches. As a guide, Bugs can also tell you that you need to lighten up and laugh a little more.

Dinosaurs

Dinosaurs existed 65 million years ago, right? But their existence is still acknowledged today. When you're dreaming about a dinosaur chasing you, something big and ugly may be haunting you from the distant past. Maybe something scared you when you were little, and the memory is still in your subconscious. Just like the long-lost dinosaurs of prehistoric times, this fear still commands attention. Your fear could be holding you back and not allowing you to grow.

Donald Duck

You know how Donald is always annoyed at his nephews for something? Well, if you are dreaming of Donald Duck, perhaps you are getting frustrated too easily. If every little thing is bothering you, try to relax. Take a deep breath, and ask yourself if whatever is making you frustrated is really that important.

Ghost

A ghost in a dream can represent old thoughts or ideas. You probably don't even know you still have these thoughts. Maybe you became friends with someone you used to dislike, but you're still thinking of the things about her that bothered you. Let go!

Glenda, the Good Witch

"There's no place like home — " If you are dreaming of Glenda, it can mean that you are looking for some help and advice. Glenda might be pointing you in the direction of home, just like she does for Dorothy in *The Wonderful Wizard of Oz*. She can represent a good friend who is a great listener and always knows the right thing to say.

Loch Ness Monster

The Loch Ness Monster lives in a deep lake, and few people have ever seen it. If you are dreaming of this creature, you might have a hidden talent that you are uncomfortable showing to the world. Perhaps you love to sing, but you're nervous about appearing in the talent show. You might be afraid that others will make fun of you or not take you seriously.

Mickey Mouse

M-I-C-K-E-Y. If you encounter Mickey in a dream, he is telling you that magic is possible. He represents creativity, fun, and play. Mickey is also the ultimate good guy. He teaches you that politeness is a good character trait.

Monsters

It sometimes seems like there are monsters that lurk in the dark, especially when you're trying to fall asleep! Monsters in a dream can represent the negative thoughts or emotions you have. They can also indicate that there are negative things around you. The way you face the monster in the dream usually mirrors how you face it in everyday life. When you wake up, take a deep breath, and think about how you can turn the negatives into positives. It's also a great idea to talk to your parents about a scary dream like this, especially if it keeps coming back.

Snoopy

Snoopy is a dreamer — whether he's thinking about pouncing on an unsuspecting Lucy, or flying a plane as the Red Baron. Dreaming of Snoopy tells you that you should use your imagination and hold on to your dreams.

Star Wars

Dreaming of Darth Vader, Princess Leia, or Chewbacca the Wookie? All of the characters from these movies represent good conquering evil, or light triumphing over dark.

Unicorn

The unicorn is like no other creature in the world, so dreaming of a unicorn can point to your unique qualities and abilities. "Dare to be different" is the message of unicorn. Because a unicorn has a beautiful horn on its forehead that points the way, it speaks of your rare psychic powers that can be used to guide you.

Winnie-the-Pooh

When you think of Pooh, what comes to mind? A loving friend? Someone who is always patient and kind? That's exactly what Pooh represents.

Chapter 8

Food and Drink:

I don't even LIKE liver —
why was I eating it in my dream?

*A*re you hungry for a big piece of cake with a cold glass of milk? Can't figure out why you're dreaming of chocolate when your favorite flavor is vanilla? This chapter will help you unlock the refrigerator door and tell you just what dreaming about certain foods can mean.

Apple

An apple in a dream can signify wisdom. The expression "An apple a day keeps the doctor away" is true in dreams as well, as apples can represent good health. So get a MacIntosh or Delicious and start crunching!

Bread

Bread represents the life-giving force that makes you healthy, wealthy and wise. Did you ever hear money called *bread* or *dough*? Dreaming about bread can indicate that some money is coming your way! Did someone play the lottery this week?!

Cake

A cake stands for the product of your creativity. Perhaps you worked on an art project that took all year and you finally

completed it. A dream may contain a cake to say, "that was a job well done". A layer cake in a dream may remind you of a very interesting person with whom you talked. It could be a reminder of a sleepover when you and your best friend stayed up talking all night!

Chocolate

Some people dream about chocolate even when they are awake! But chocolate in a dream signifies comfort and love.

Eating

I'm starving! Dreaming about eating doesn't necessarily mean it's time for a midnight snack. It can indicate that you are taking in (digesting) information that you just received.

Eggs

I'll have mine sunny-side up, please! Eggs mean that a lot of good opportunities have come your way. A broken egg can indicate that you didn't get to take advantage of an opportunity. A sunny-side-up egg means there is a great opportunity awaiting you.

Meat

Cutting into a piece of meat in a dream can mean that you are getting to the heart of something. And that certain something is very important to you. Maybe you had a talk with your brother or sister and you feel that you're really coming to understand one another.

Milk

Whole, two-percent, or skim, dreaming of milk can signify that you are nurturing someone close to you or that someone is nurturing you. Spilling your milk may mean that you lost an important and meaningful opportunity.

Popcorn

Eating popcorn can mean that you are sitting back and enjoying a movie — the dream you are in. It may mention that there is a kernel of truth in the motion picture of your dream and that you are enjoying and digesting the information. If you are popping popcorn, you might be forming big, exciting thoughts in your mind.

Soda

An ice-cold soda can be a great refresher, right? Dreaming of soda can remind you of an event that was great. Perhaps it was an amazing party with friends, or a fun afternoon in the park with your family. Soda can also represent an innovative idea.

Spaghetti

Spaghetti in a dream can indicate that you were involved in a long, involved conversation. It could be a perfectly 'cooked' one, or one that was long, stringy, and messy.

Turkey

Gobble, gobble! Dreaming of a turkey can mean that you are about to receive a gift. As a traditional symbol of Thanksgiving, it can also mean that you are appreciating what you have.

Vitamins

A dream that contains vitamins may actually mean that you need some in your real life (amazing, right?). Vitamins build strong bodies, so eating a handful in a dream can tell you that you often wish you were a stronger person.

Chapter 9

Potpourri:

And I was captured by aliens and taken aboard their spaceship —

I was in a bubble bath, and then suddenly I was shopping for clothes. Huh? Did you ever have one of those dreams where nothing makes sense? What is your dream trying to tell you? This chapter contains random symbols that you might encounter in your dreams.

Bathing

If you are dreaming of lounging in a tub, you might need to take it a bit easier. Bathing signifies that you want a break from stress and worry. If you are in a bubble bath, you probably really need to take it easy — a bubble bath indicates that you need some heavy-duty pampering.

Books

If you're dreaming of books, you might be about to discover some new knowledge. Check out the title of the book — it will probably give you a clue as to what you're about to learn.

Chasing

Don't you hate that dream where the bad guy is chasing you? This is a symbol that's not too hard to figure out. If you are being chased, you're probably trying to escape a person or situation that you find unpleasant. If you are the one doing the chasing, you might be feeling anxious or angry towards someone or pursuing a goal that is just out of reach. Don't give up!

Clothes

Did you ever have a dream where you're dressed in an outfit that doesn't match? That IS a nightmare! Different pieces of clothing can symbolize different ideas:

Jeans: Wearing tight jeans in a dream can mean that something within you feels restricted and too controlled.

Shirt: Buttoning up a shirt can mean that you are concerned about the image you project to the world — you don't want to reveal too much of your heart.

Shoes: Remember when you read that your feet bind you to the earth? (See *Feet*, page 34) Well, your shoes do the same thing. If you're walking around in uncomfortable shoes, it can mean that you're not comfortable with yourself in the world. If you have lost your shoes, you might be losing touch with the earth and reality.

Colors

Colors can give you clues about your mood in a dream. Different colors have different meanings:

Blue: Dreaming of blue means that you are content.

Green: Green is the color of healing and nature.

Purple: If you dream about purple, that's great! It's the color of psychic power and intuition (See, we told you this dream stuff could tell you things you never knew!).

Red: The color red means that you are very passionate about something.

Yellow: Cheery yellow means that you have a positive outlook on life and intelligence.

Computer

Who wouldn't dream about a computer — you probably use one a lot during the day. Dreaming of a computer can mean that you are worried about your learning ability. For example, if your computer crashes, you might think that you are going to forget everything you've learned. Maybe you've been studying for a big test, but you're not sure if you are actually absorbing the information.

Doll

Dreaming of a doll can mean that you are focusing on your early childhood. You might be thinking of your mother and the way she took care of you when you were little (even if you can't remember it!). A Barbie doll might signify that you are not feeling good about yourself and are comparing yourself to others.

Eyeglasses

Dreaming of eyeglasses means that you need to take a closer look at a situation before acting. Perhaps you want to join a new sports team, but you haven't really thought about the time it will require. Look before you leap!

Falling

This is another common dream — but it's a scary one! If you are falling in a dream, it might mean that you are losing control of something. Perhaps you're not doing too well in school, or you're not feeling too good about yourself. If you have it over and over again, it can mean that you're really bothered by this loss. This is a great dream to share with your parents — maybe they can help you figure out how to recover what you've lost

Flying

If you dream about flying, it can mean that you want to be free. Maybe you feel tied down by too many things — dance practice, soccer tournaments, and homework. Enjoy this dream — what could be more fun than soaring above the earth like a bird?!

Gloves

Wearing gloves in a dream can mean that you are protecting yourself from something. Are you covering up your true personality? Or are you holding back about telling your friends exactly how you feel about something?

Jewelry

Dreaming of a five-carat diamond ring? Jewelry is a symbol of both beauty and radiance. Diamonds, which radiate light, may suggest that it's time to show your inner light to the world. Emeralds can heal the heart and signify faith and hope. Rubies,  with their deep red color, signify that you are passionate about something. Pearls stand for wisdom and can reflect how something beautiful can come out of an irritating situation (oysters form pearls around grains of sand). And turquoise is showing you the opportunity to open up your lines of communication.

Light

Light in a dream can mean that you are getting a clear vision about something. Perhaps you can't figure out that last math problem, but you just thought of a solution. Or you can't decide which of two outfits to wear to the big dance, but you thought of a third that would be even better. Light in a dream might also mean that you are about to encounter a ray of light or situation that will brighten your life.

Los Angeles

Do you dream of being a star in this city? Los Angeles is the center of entertainment and is the home of a lot of special celebrities, so if you find yourself in it, you might be thinking about showing the world how special and unique you are.

Lost

Don't you hate that dream where you can't figure out where you are? Scary! If you are lost in your dream, it might mean that you have lost some part of yourself. Maybe you're having a tough time at home, and you can't seem to enjoy anything. Share this dream with your parents — they can probably help you figure out what's missing.

Music

Music in a dream can mean that it's time for you to get up and dance. You need to have fun! If you hear a familiar song, you might be getting a message about something — for example, if "Girlfriend" is playing, maybe you want to let that special boy know exactly how you feel! See if the other things in your dream can clue you in to what this special message is.

New York

Have you suddenly found yourself on the streets of this amazing city? If you have, you might be seeing yourself in the future. New York is known for its wonderful theaters, amazing businesses, and is the center

for financial markets. Perhaps your career will be in one of these areas.

Pen/Pencil

Using a pen or pencil in a dream can signify that you're making an impact with your words. A pen represents a more permanent situation or relationship, while a pencil can mean that your words — or relationship — won't last and can be 'erased.'

Piano

If a piano appears in your dream, you might be thinking about how to be more balanced. Since your right hand and your left hand have to work together to make beautiful music, you could be thinking of how to be both creative and logical. (See *Music*, page 58)

Pillow

Are you dreaming of a soft fluffy pillow? If you are, you probably need to relax a bit more. A pillow signifies that your mind is overworked and needs to slow down. Try to take a few minutes each day to let your mind wander around unfocused.

School

Dreaming about school should seem almost natural—you probably spend most of your waking hours there. If you are dreaming of school, you're thinking about the things you need to learn in order to grow. An elementary school can represent the basic knowledge you learned as a younger kid. Dreaming of high school

means that you are learning about your emotions and feelings. And dreaming of college can signify that you're ready to learn about what you need to know to succeed in life.

Vacuum Cleaner

Is it time to clean out your brain? If you are dreaming of a vacuum cleaner, it might be. Just like vacuum cleaners suck up dirt and dust, maybe it's time for you to clear your head of negative thoughts. Or it may simply be time to clean your room!

Chapter 10

Tying it all together:
Symbols, metaphors, and more

Whew! Bet your brain is swimming from reading about all those symbols. But finding what a symbol can mean is just the beginning—you need to know how to relate it to your everyday life. Be patient—with each dream you recall and try to decipher, you'll get better at it. Sometimes dreams can become clearer over a period of time—especially if you are having the same or similar dreams over and over and over. Remember, you want not only find the symbols in your dreams—the things that actually appear—but the metaphors—the details and ideas that accompany the symbols. Take another look at the introduction for a more in-depth explanation of the difference between symbols and metaphors.

Let's say you have a dream where you are hanging out with your friends, but in it, your fingernails are really long. Perhaps your subconscious is telling you that you need to defend yourself against something that a friend is doing. You might not even know what it is that could hurt you, but your subconscious does!

Maybe you have a dream where you are reclining on a pillow in a beautiful green room. A-ha! Since a pillow can symbolize that you're overworked and the color green suggests healing, it can mean that you really need to slow down before you get sick!

There are a lot more symbols you might find in your dreams that we haven't even talked about here. Check out your local library for some books that can further help you understand your dreams. And keep listening to your dreams — you never know WHAT they might tell you!

Index to Symbols

Good Dreams _____

_____
_____
_____
_____
_____
_____
_____
_____
_____
_____
_____
_____
_____
_____
_____
_____
_____
_____
_____
_____
_____
_____
_____
_____

Bad Dreams

Good Dreams _____

_____

_____

_____

_____

_____

_____

_____

_____

_____

_____

_____

_____

_____

_____

_____

_____

_____

_____

_____

_____

_____

_____

_____

_____

Bad Dreams _____

_____

_____

_____

_____

_____

_____

_____

_____

_____

_____

_____

_____

_____

_____

_____

_____

_____

_____

_____

_____

_____

_____

_____

Good Dreams _____

_____
_____
_____
_____
_____
_____
_____
_____
_____
_____
_____
_____
_____
_____
_____
_____
_____
_____
_____
_____
_____
_____
_____
_____
_____
_____
_____

Bad Dreams _____

_____
_____
_____
_____
_____
_____
_____
_____
_____
_____
_____
_____
_____
_____
_____
_____
_____
_____
_____
_____
_____
_____
_____
_____
_____
_____

Good Dreams _____

_____

_____

_____

_____

_____

_____

_____

_____

_____

_____

_____

_____

_____

_____

_____

_____

_____

_____

_____

_____

_____

_____

_____

_____

Dedication

Dedicated to the memory of our mom Patricia Bley,

who both inspired us and encouraged us to follow our dreams

With love,

Mike, Gail, Jim, and Tom